PLATFORM PAPERS

QUARTERLY ESSAYS ON THE PERFORMING ARTS FROM CURRENCY HOUSE

No. 48
August 2016

CURRENCY HOUSE

Platform Papers Partners

We acknowledge with gratitude our Partners in continuing support of Platform Papers and its mission to widen understanding of performing arts practice and encourage change when it is needed:

Gillian Appleton
Neil Armfield, AO
Anita Luca Belgiorno Nettis Foundation
Jane Bowen, AM
Jane Bridge
Katharine Brisbane, AM
Elizabeth Butcher, AM
Penny Chapman
Robert Connolly
Peter Cooke, OAM
Rowena Cowley and Dr Richard Letts, AM
Sally Crawford
Michael J. Crouch, AO
Wesley Enoch
Ian Enright
Ferrier Hodgson
Larry Galbraith
Tony Grierson
Gail Hambly
Wayne Harrison, AM
Campbell Hudson
Professors Bruce King AC and Denise Bradley, AC
Justice François Kunc
Peter Lee
Peter Lowry, OAM and Carolyn Lowry, OAM
Michael Lynch, CBE, AM
Roderick H. McGeoch, AO
David Marr
Harold Mitchell, AC, AO
Joanna Murray-Smith
Helen O'Neil
Martin Portus
Positive Solutions
Lesley Power
Professor William Purcell
Queensland Performing Arts Centre Trust
Geoffrey Rush, AC
Seaborn Broughton Walford Foundation
Sky Foundation
Dr Merilyn Sleigh
Maisy Stapleton
Augusta Supple
Andrew Upton
Rachel Ward, AM and Bryan Brown, AM
Kim Williams, AM
Professor Di Yerbury, AM

To them and to all subscribers and Friends of Currency House we extend our grateful thanks.

Platform Papers

Readers' Forum

Readers' responses to our previous essays are posted on our website. Contributions to the conversation (250 to 2000 words) may be emailed to info@currencyhouse.org.au. The Editor welcomes opinion and criticism in the interest of healthy debate but reserves the right to monitor where necessary.

Platform Papers, quarterly essays on the performing arts, is published every February, May, August and November and is available through bookshops, by subscription and on line in paper or electronic version. For details see our website at www.currencyhouse.org.au.

WHEN THE GOAL POSTS MOVE:

Patronage, power and resistance in Australian cultural policy 2013–16

BEN ELTHAM

ABOUT THE AUTHOR

Ben Eltham is a journalist and researcher based in Melbourne. He is currently a Lecturer in the School of Communications and Creative Arts at Deakin University and the National Affairs Correspondent for *New Matilda*. Eltham studied cultural policy at Western Sydney University's Institute for Culture and Society, and has worked as a freelance arts journalist and critic, producer and festival director in Newcastle, Brisbane and Melbourne. He is a Fellow of the Centre for Policy Development, an independent public policy think-tank for long-term research fellows.

Eltham writes regularly about Australian culture and politics for the popular media and publishes in academic journals on cultural policy, social media and communication theory.

ACKNOWLEDGEMENTS

This Platform Paper was commissioned by Katharine Brisbane, whose towering contribution to Australia's cultural life is attested to by the fact that this is the forty-eighth Platform Paper. Julian Meyrick kindly read a draft and provided much-needed feedback, as did editor Robin Derricourt. Deb Verhoeven has been a huge source of encouragement and support. Justin O'Connor has also been a mentor, and offered the opportunity to present a guest lecture to his Masters students at Monash University, which allowed me to develop my thinking. The journalism that informed the paper was commissioned by supportive editors at *Arts Hub*, *New Matilda*, *Crikey*, *Overland, Meanjin* and the *Guardian*, especially Marni Cordell, Catri Menzies-Pike, Jason Whittaker, Deborah Stone, Cassidy Knowlton, Sophie Cunningham, Jacinda Woodhead and Steph Harmon. My ideas regarding the commemoration of Anzac were first developed for a research symposium on the Centenary of Anzac held at Deakin on 16 April 2015, hosted by the UNESCO Chair, Cultural Diversity and Social Justice. I thank David Tittensor for the chance to present my findings to Australian and Turkish colleagues; and Peter Stanley, who offered generous feedback on the day.

The main source of my inspiration has been the many hundreds of artists and cultural workers to whom I have spoken over the past fifteen years, and who have shaped my understanding of the complexity and diversity of Australian culture. There are too many to name but I would particularly like to thank Alison Croggon, Alon Ilsar, Angela Conquet, Beau McCafferty, Ben Ball, Bryan Mason, Caro McDonald, Chris O'Neill, Collette Brennan, David McDonald, David Pledger, David Ryding, Emily Sexton, Esther Anatolitis, George Megalogenis, Gillian Gardiner, Gillian Terzis, Helen Marcou, Jade Lillie, James O'Brien, Jane Howard, Jeff Khan, Joel Zika, John Wardle, Jonathan Green, Julie Dyson, Kath Quigley, Karina Sedgwick, Kris Stewart, Lawrence English, Leigh Tabrett, Lou Oppenheim, Lucy Guerin, Marcel Dorney, Marcus Westbury, Marni Jackson, Neal Harvey, Nicholas Pickard, Nicole Beyer, Norm Horton, Pilar Kassat, Rachel Healy, Richard Watts, Sabrina D'Angelo, Sarah Moynihan, Sophie Hyde, Stu Watters, Tai Snaith, Tamara Winikoff, Tom Doig, Wesley Enoch, Zane Trow and Zola Affley.

In the past decade Arts ministers George Brandis, Peter Garrett, Simon Crean, Tony Burke and Mitch Fifield have all answered questions or granted interviews with me. Despite my frequent provocations, I'd like to thank them too.

1. Black Friday, May 2016

On Friday 13 May 2016, the Australia Council for the Arts released the results of that agency's 'Four Year Organisations' grants. The result was a bloodbath: 65 organisations were defunded, and more than a hundred that applied were also unsuccessful. The arts sector dubbed it 'Black Friday'.[1]

Some of the most famous arts companies in the country missed out. The Australian Design Centre has a 50-year history supporting Australian design and craft.[2] The literary magazine *Meanjin* was the place where A.A. Phillips first coined the phrase 'the cultural cringe' in his seminal essay.[3] The cuts punished organisations that support younger artists, in literature, dance and theatre, such as Melbourne's Next Wave festival, the nation's premier event for young and emerging artists, and Express Media, the publisher of *Voiceworks* magazine. Other casualties included Adelaide's Vitalstatistix and Slingsby, Melbourne's Centre for Contemporary Photography, and north Queensland's Jute Theatre.

The defunding of a slew of Australia's best-known smaller arts companies was due to a decision made by the Abbott Government's arts minister, George Brandis, who had taken $105 million in funding from the Australia Council a year before. Funding cuts bit deep. The decision came in addition to $87 million slashed from the Arts portfolio in 2014. Further cuts of $52.5 million were handed down in December 2015. All told, according to the Australian Labor Party's Mark Dreyfus, approximately $300 million has been cut from federal cultural funding by the Coalition.

Before the 2013 election, arts funding had been a more-or-less bipartisan policy area, supported by both major parties. The Coalition did not release an arts policy in the 2013 campaign, nor did it commit to specific cuts. Indeed, George Brandis gave an enthusiastic speech at the Casula Powerhouse pledging the Coalition's support for the grand vision of the arts.[4] That bipartisanship disappeared in the newly ideological environment of the new Abbott Government. The Coalition didn't just slash the Australia Council's funding. It launched a new attack on arm's length arts funding itself—a principle that has enjoyed four decades of bipartisan support. Why did George Brandis and the Coalition do this? What accounts for this assault on the cultural sphere?

This essay is an attempt to tell that story, and to question what it means for culture in Australia. I shall start by explaining a little about my method and craft, and then examine the sorry story of arts funding in the most recent parliament. Then I will make some remarks about what this story tells us about power in Australian society. There has been push and pull: action and resistance. Australian culture is being attacked by political actors, beholden to an ideology of privatising the cultural space. But if there are troubling realities, there are also opportunities: a possibility of arguing for the greater cultural good. I will end with a call to arms to defend and expand the cultural sphere of Australia.

2. Methods

Culture, as Raymond Williams famously declared, is one of the 'two or three most complicated words in the English language.'[5] We use the word in many different ways. There is a sense of culture as a set of symbolic and social interactions amongst a people—this, very roughly, is the sense in which anthropologists use the word.[6] Here the word 'culture' is a synonym for collective conduct. This is the sense in which corporations or football teams can be said to have 'a culture' (a 'culture of greed'; a 'winning culture').

We also use of the word 'culture' to denote works of art and literature. As Williams pointed out, this is the idea of culture as 'the independent and abstract noun which describes the works and practices of intellectual and especially artistic activity.' Even in the early 1980s, Williams thought that 'this seems often now the most widespread use: culture is music, literature, painting and sculpture, theatre and film.'[7] And that is the meaning of the word 'culture' that I will use throughout this essay. Further, I will use the words 'art' and 'culture' more or less interchangeably. There is a certain sloppiness to this conflation, but it suits my purposes to emphasise the unity of artistic and cultural expression. This is so when it comes to the fields of human creativity that take in what we sometimes call the 'high arts', but equally true for the more commercial and technological forms of artmaking, such as gaming, design, photography, 'digital media' and the like.

I approach the field of culture as both a participant and an observer. For the past decade, I've inquired into Australian culture as a journalist and an academic researcher. I've also worked as a festival director, a creative producer and a freelance writer. In these capacities I've come to know well the peculiar joys and fears of artists: the sorrows of poverty and the ecstasies of transformative craft.[8]

Most particularly, I've covered Australian culture as a journalist. It's worth explaining a little about what this has involved. The arts journalist is, quite simply, a journalist who reports on and covers the arts. In the Australian context, this is a 'round' or a 'beat' that is essentially a species of business journalism, taking the arts and cultural industries as its subject area. Over the years, I've covered stories about industry trends—especially the all-conquering tide of digital technology—but also the actions and proclivities of various arts ministers, the rise and fall of big music festivals, the pay of artistic directors, and the health or sickness of various art forms (the theatre is always dying, as the playwright Brendan Behan lamented).

The arts journalist can be distinguished from other writers who devote their work to the arts. While she certainly needs to go out and see art, she is not chiefly a critic. The critic sees and judges work, hopefully sensitively and knowledgably; the arts journalist is more interested in what the work tells us about underlying power structures. Nor is the arts journalist (solely, at any rate) an essayist or art historian. While she might occasionally write at considerable length in the pursuit of a particular investigation, her customary output remains the report.

Like other forms of journalism, arts journalism is topical and immediate. It tends towards the sensationalist at times but it also plays a critical role scrutinising a small and often incestuous industry. In a cultural milieu where powerful artistic directors and funding bodies can swiftly punish critics, arts journalists are perhaps the only people allowed or even encouraged to ask difficult questions of arts ministers, funding bodies and cultural institutions. They are certainly amongst the few individuals who can expect formal, on-the-record answers to their questions.

As it turns out, there are plenty of difficult questions worth asking. Arts journalism may well be a contracting niche in a sickly mediascape, but the past few years have been something of a golden age for the news round. Surprising and important events have kept happening. There has been plenty to uncover. That's given people like me lots to report on.

3. False dawn: March 2013

One of those events came on a warm Canberra day in March 2013, when Arts Minister Simon Crean gathered many of Australia's best-known artists and cultural leaders together to launch *Creative Australia*, the nation's first cultural policy in 19 years.[9]

Crean's policy came late in the life of the Gillard Government. Six years in the making, *Creative Australia* had only narrowly managed to win the support of embattled Prime Minister Julia Gillard. In a government plagued by internal unrest and a political landscape dominated by big-picture issues like climate change and the National Disability Insurance Scheme, cultural policy had been stop-start—mainly stop. Labor insiders say the policy was finally green-lit in February 2013 after a confrontation between Crean and Gillard, in which Crean threatened to resign.

Australian cultural policy has often been like that. Fragmented by history and bureaucratic diktat, many federal government policies impinge on culture. But there has been little coordination or even understanding between the various arms of cultural policy—between the states and the Commonwealth, for instance; or between broadcasting policy and the broader cultural sector; or between innovation policy addressed to the natural sciences and cultural policy addressed to arts institutions—or between universities and everyone else.[10]

Australia's cultural policy debate is blinkered in many respects. It is often profoundly insular; only dimly aware of the achievements and events of policymakers in the rest of the world, or of Australia's not-inconsiderable place in them. It is ahistorical, often taking little account of the temporal development of contemporary policy. And it is constrained by arbitrary conceptual boundaries, particularly when judged against public policy in the main.

For instance, the issue of arts funding currently dominates public discussions of cultural policy. This means the current narrative is skewed towards questions of scarcity, rather than acknowledgment of the ubiquity and value of cultural expression. There is not enough funding to go around. There is 'unfunded excellence'—the felicitous phrase dreamed up by Angus James and Gabrielle Trainor in their review of the Australia Council carried out in 2012.[11] Funding is being cut or withdrawn. Such discussions are often presented as part and parcel of a federal budget deficit, in which there is too much spending and not enough revenue. In that context, cuts to the arts are inevitable, as an exercise of 'budget repair.' And yet there are huge swathes of culture that are not funded by the government, and have never been.

Crean's *Creative Australia* was an attempt to address these inconsistencies, bringing the various strands of cultural policy into a slightly more harmonious whole. Long in gestation and in the end short on detail, it painted in broad brushstrokes, and often seemed slightly sketchy on specifics. Labor's vision for Australian culture was expansive. 'Culture is created by us and defines us,' it proclaimed. 'It is the embodiment of the distinctive values, traditions and beliefs that make being Australian in the twenty-first century unique—democratic, diverse, adaptive and grounded in one of the world's oldest living civilisations.'

While the sector welcomed the rhetoric, the real enthusiasm was attached to the policy's funding boost. There was $236 million in new money, including $75 million to the Australia Council to support 'unfunded excellence'. Australia Council reform was a key goal of the policy.

'Unfunded excellence' really meant 'more money for arts grants', and that was what many in the sector were so supportive of. For the first time in two decades, Australia had a national cultural policy that saw culture as something worthy of government investment. Artists and industry figures welcomed it when I reported on this at the time. Malthouse's Jo Porter told me that 'one of the exciting things of the speech yesterday was the sense that creativity is part of our national culture [...] that was incredibly heartening; it was fantastic to hear that from the Minister.' Rick Heath of the Australian Performing Arts Centres Association was particularly pleased by the fact of a politician actually speaking up for the value of culture. 'It's great to hear a political leader speak and advocate convincingly about the value of the art,' Heath said. 'The money is of less importance than having someone show some leadership in the cultural sector.'[12]

But 'leadership' would turn out to be an ominous word—especially for a Labor government about to tear itself apart over precisely that issue. Just a fortnight after launching the national cultural policy, Crean blew himself up in an extraordinary leadership challenge. Frustrated at the guerrilla campaign of leaks and media backgrounding being waged by Kevin Rudd and his supporters against Julia Gillard, Crean called a snap media conference to announce he was moving a party room motion for a vote on the ALP parliamentary leadership. The challenge disintegrated after Kevin Rudd refused to run for Labor's leadership. In farcical scenes, Gillard was then obliged to sack Crean and several of his front-bench supporters.[13]

The episode came to encapsulate all that was dysfunctional about the federal Labor Government of the Rudd-Gillard years—an administration in which factional politics and personal ambition conspired to defeat sound public policy, or even straightforward political self-interest. As a result, the Arts Minister who had developed *Creative Australia* and ushered it through cabinet was unceremoniously dumped. The ministerial staffers in Crean's office, some of whom had been working on the cultural policy for years, were given just a few minutes to empty their desks and clear out their personal belongings.[14]

The Crean implosion signified much about Labor's faltering commitment to culture and the arts. To its credit, it did implement most of the key planks of *Creative Australia* before being bundled out of office in September 2013. Under replacement Arts Minister Tony Burke, the funding for *Creative Australia* was delivered, the Australia Council's governing legislation was re-written, and new money to the cultural sector started to flow. On the eve of the election that would elect Tony Abbott and the Coalition, there was cautious optimism across much of the sector, mixed with trepidation about what a Coalition government might do.

4. 'The capacity of the Minister to give directions ...': September 2013

For those reading the tea leaves, there was much to be concerned about. An article in the *Australian* on 23 May had already foreseen a much colder climate for the arts under Abbott.

'The arts sector should prepare for a change of government on 14 September and be ready to drop fuzzy justifications for unfunding, according to a prominent government lobbyist,' The *Australian*'s Matthew Westwood wrote.

> *The head of Labor-aligned government relations company Hawker Britton, Justin Di Lollo, said the arts sector should be talking to Coalition politicians at every level, and learn to speak their language.*
>
> *'There is an element of 'lost in translation,' Mr Di Lollo said yesterday. 'It's not because the Liberal Party doesn't understand the arts sector. I think it's because the arts sector hasn't been communicating in a way that's appropriate to the Coalition's priorities.'*

Mr Di Lollo has been invited to speak next week at an annual arts marketing summit organised by the Australia Council, the federal Government's distributor of arts funding. [...]

Funding under a Coalition government was not necessarily at risk but the arts had to emphasise the economic benefits and job creation rather than the 'inherent' value of culture. He advised arts professionals to steer discussion away from community outcomes and towards the enrichment of individuals from cultural experiences.

As the year lengthened, Labor's re-election prospects dissolved in the chaos of the Rudd-Gillard civil war. Policy limped on, even as the Government tore itself apart. Close to the election, Labor introduced the Australia Council reform bill.[15] As Opposition Arts spokesperson, George Brandis attempted to sabotage it in the Senate, inserting an amendment that would have allowed the Arts Minister of the day to veto Australia Council funding decisions. The amendment was voted down, but it was an early sign that Brandis would take a far more activist role when it came to arts funding decisions. 'I was concerned about aspects of the Australia Council Bill which would have imposed new limitations on the capacity of the Minister to give directions to the Australia Council, in areas other than particular programs or particular funding,' he said in a media interview in August 2013.[16]

There was also a pointer to future priorities in the use of that troubling word, 'excellence.' 'The Coalition views the arts as one of the principal arenas in which Australians strive for and achieve excellence,' Brandis said in the 2013 campaign's debate on arts policy with Tony Burke in western Sydney. 'The pursuit of excellence across all of the artistic genres will be the central value of cultural policy under a Coalition Government.'[17]

5. 'Vicious ingratitude': The Biennale boycott

The Coalition won the 2013 election, and George Brandis became the Attorney-General and Arts Minister. He was not in office for long before the first major controversy of his tenure blew up at the Biennale of Sydney. This was an artist boycott of the festival, in protest against the relationship of a sponsor to Australian immigration policy. A key philanthropic funder of the Biennale was Transfield Holdings, a family company run by the Belgiorno-Nettis brothers. Transfield Holdings held shares in Transfield Services, a company with a lucrative federal government contract to run the controversial immigration detention centre on Manus Island, where a riot had recently led to the murder of an asylum seeker, Reza Berati.[18]

From a small beginning—the boycott began with a single letter by a Sydney academic named Matthew Kiem—the boycott snowballed into a major media circus. More than thirty prominent artists eventually signed an open letter against Transfield and its chairman, Luca Belgiorno-Nettis, writing that the sponsorship of the Biennale formed 'a chain of connections that link to human suffering.' Engulfed in negative media attention, Belgiorno-Nettis resigned as the Biennale's chair.

The Biennale imbroglio sent shockwaves through

Australia's closely interwoven arts community. The decision of well-known artists to boycott a major visual arts festival, and to actively target a major sponsor for political reasons, upset the received wisdoms of arts management. The boycott and its subsequent blowback exposed Belgiorno-Nettis and the Biennale's well-known but unpopular artistic director, Julianna Engberg, to considerable criticism. It also attracted plenty of opprobrium on the artists themselves, whom right-wing critics attacked for their hypocrisy in boycotting a corporate sponsor while taking money from the federal government that had commissioned the asylum seeker camps in the first place.

But the real blowback was social. To the wealthy patrons used to deference and gratitude from the cultural activities they helped fund, the backlash was shocking. In an interview with the ABC in March 2014, a bewildered Belgiorno-Nettis complained of being 'vilified' by 'guerrilla activists.' The wounded philanthropist told the ABC's listeners that 'these guerrilla activists [...] are accusing myself, my family, the Biennale and the Transfield brand as ethically indefensible for what we're doing,' he said, citing the support of both major parties for Australia's tough policy of mandatory detention.[19] But what Belgiorno-Nettis really seemed upset about was the fact that artists would question the ethics of the hand that fed them. (The feeling was understandable. Luca's father Franco had founded the Biennale of Sydney in 1973 and Transfield had been its major sponsor and partner ever since.) Long-time artistic director Leo Schofield in the *Sydney Morning Herald* also hit back at the artists: 'How arts organisations find the money to pay for events is not the artists' business.' Indeed,

Schofield added, 'this is a gross example of people exhibiting self-importance that they haven't earned.'[20] But it was Malcolm Turnbull, then the Communications Minister, who topped them all. 'The sheer vicious ingratitude of it all!' he exclaimed in a radio interview.[21]

George Brandis gave few interviews as Arts Minister, and it's impossible to know to what degree the Biennale controversy shaped his thinking as a policymaker. But it's clear the boycott played a major role in what came later. Brandis immediately foreshadowed a new policy stipulation that would strip arts organisations of government funding should they refuse corporate sponsorship, and he wrote to the Australia Council's board to direct it to come up with a policy to that effect. Australia Council chairman Rupert Myer wrote back, promising to look into it. But the damage had been done: the seeds of a later whirlwind had been sown.

6. The origins of 'excellence': 1974

The Australia Council is a Keynesian institution. Its founding philosophies were welfarist and elitist, and its true founder was not in fact Whitlam, but rather the powerful Commonwealth bureaucrat H.C. Nugget Coombs, who saw in a proposal for a national arts funding body an opportunity to bring culture to the masses, and to advance the cause of Australian public life. It was Coombs who sold Menzies on the idea of a funding body in celebration of the visit of the young Queen Elizabeth to Australia in 1954: this was the Australian Elizabethan Theatre Trust, and it would dispense limited amounts of public funding to ostensibly high-art endeavours such as opera, ballet and orchestral music.

Coombs was Canberra's most active and effective bureaucrat throughout much of the postwar period, and he had played a key role in Chifley's plans for national reconstruction. Taking his cue from Keynes' establishment of the Arts Council of England in June 1945, Coombs became convinced of the need for Australia to support cultural reconstruction in a similar manner.

Coombs' original vision for the Australia Council was torn straight from the pages of Matthew Arnold: its purpose would be 'to ensure the best is encouraged and those who produce it are given the greatest opportunity to achieve the highest quality of which they are capable.' The agency would address a critical market failure in Australian society: the exodus of artists to overseas careers, the 'thinness of professional practice,' 'a lack of professional organisations capable of stimulating the performance or protecting the rights of artists.'[22] The new Commonwealth arts body would remedy these defects, allowing Australian artists to ply their trade in their home nation, and giving citizens access to a distinctively national culture.

Whitlam took this incipient Keynesianism and elevated it into something grander: the vision of a Commonwealth body that would fund the arts not merely for the edification of the under-cultured masses, but for the greater good of the nation and the value of culture itself. When introducing the Australia Council bill to the House of Representatives in 1974, he inscribed the purpose of the agency squarely in terms of supporting artists. Indeed, the speech could almost be seen as an apology to the Australian 'ex-pats', the writers, artists and performers who had left the continent for a chance to make art overseas:

> *Artists have an essential role to play in our society. No-one can imagine a mature civilisation without their contribution [...] The Government believes they should be able to work in their own country secure in the knowledge that the community and the Government place a high value on their contribution to our way of life [...] We want to ensure that our greatest artists remain in Australia and prosper in*

> *Australia, and that the whole Australian community is the richer for their presence [...] I believe that, through the measures in this Bill, we will create greater artistic opportunities for all talented Australians. We shall be offering to all who by birth or choice have made this country their home the prospect of enriching their lives through participation in or appreciation of the arts.*[23]

Whitlam's Australia Council would be a fundamentally public institution. As Keynes and Coombs had envisaged, it would correct the market failure that had made it so difficult for artists to ply their trade. Indeed, as Keynes had argued in 1936, the arts 'cannot be successfully carried on if they depend on the motive of profit and financial success.'[24] The Australia Council would support artists, above all, and its role would be to help them make a frugal living while they created work.

But if the artist was central to Whitlam's vision of the Australia Council the years since have not been kind to her fundamental role. Over time, the Australia Council turned into an agency that spent the majority of its budget funding a select coterie of favoured institutions: the 28 major performing arts companies that still account for more than half its total budget. Once smaller companies are included, funding for organisations now accounts for more than three-quarters of the agency's spend. Support for individual artists, or small groups, represents something less than ten per cent.

The history of the Australia Council is long and fascinating, and unfortunately we do not have the space to trace it in detail here.[25] It was during the Hawke Government that many of the most important decisions were taken, including the decision to create a 'major performing arts unit' for the most important performing arts companies, including Opera Australia and the Australian Ballet. As Julian Meyrick notes in a recent article:

> *[...] in 1986 the House of Representatives' Patronage, Power and the Muse (the McLeay Report) made the fateful recommendation to establish a major organisations unit and within a few years the Performing Arts Board, as it was then, lost 80 per cent of its disbursable funds.*
>
> *This decision has been the chief structural determinant of the distribution of cultural subsidy over the last 25 years. It effectively created a two-tier system: major organisations on the one hand, smaller organisations and independent artists on the other.*[26]

The decision to give the major companies their own quasi-autonomous unit within the Australia Council, confirmed by Keating's *Creative Nation* policy, has shaped the way Australian cultural policy has been structured since. The institutional heft of the major performing arts companies continues to dominate policy discussions; as Meyrick points out, the majors-indies divide determines 'the distribution of cultural subsidy.' And the key justification for that subsidy is currently 'excellence.'

We have already encountered the word 'excellence' in this essay, courtesy of George Brandis' 2013 election debate at the Casula Powerhouse. His enthusiastic adoption of the term reflects the victory of a certain view of culture in Australia's political economy. 'Excellence', a code word, a handy signifier that equated to an unashamedly 'high art' view of culture. In policy terms it means support for the major performing arts sector. In this analysis, articulated by Brandis as about 'the great audiences', what matters in culture are the great works of the tradition. These are the canonical classics representing the pinnacle of enlightened humanity: Western orchestral music and opera, Shakespearian theatre and European old master painting. This view is not held by many artists themselves, who can be iconoclastic in their tastes. But it is widely held by Liberal politicians, by the Commonwealth arts bureaucracy and amongst the professional company directors of the corporate world who populate the boards of major cultural institutions. 'Excellence' is also an attractive value to those in the business community enamoured of neoliberal concepts like 'competition' and 'risk', as we shall explore in more detail below.

As I argued in *Overland* last year, the point about excellence was precisely *not* an artistic one.[27] No national cultural policy can coherently articulate what 'artistic excellence' even is, let alone devise a policy which procures more of it. Instead, 'excellence' was simply the name given to the policy of supporting the major companies and institutions–those big companies that attracted the support of the elite class of art-loving bank CEOs, company directors and merchant bankers. The Australia Council Review commissioned by Crean is the perfect example: it was conducted by Angus James, a merchant banker who also happened to be deputy chair of the Australian Chamber Orchestra, and Gabrielle Trainor, a company director and spin doctor who had previously sat on the board of the Sydney Symphony.[28]

With the 'excellence' narrative firmly supported by the incoming Coalition arts minister, the suspicion was always that any funding cuts implemented by the Abbott Government would be deflected from the major companies, and would instead fall on the rest of the Australia Council's client base. And that is exactly what happened.

7. The power of ministers: May 2015

Few saw the Excellence Raid of May 2015 coming. In the wake of the Biennale controversy and the funding cuts of Treasurer Joe Hockey's politically disastrous 2014 budget, anxiety in the cultural sector had abated somewhat. There were no overt warning signs. Brandis appeared content to let the Australia Council get on with the job of restructuring itself along the lines laid down by Trainor and James.

The decision handed down in Canberra on budget day in May 2015 astonished everyone with its audacity. Without a hint of warning, Brandis peremptorily moved $105 million of the Australia Council's funding out of the agency, using it to set up a ministerial slush fund. He gave this the grandiose title of the National Program for Excellence in the Arts. The Australia Council's chair, Rupert Myer, was called at about 5pm on budget day, just hours before Hockey was due to release the budget papers. The agency's CEO, Tony Grybowski, cut short a family holiday in Britain and rushed back to Sydney. The sector was gobsmacked. No-one was consulted. No-one was even told. Brandis simply announced it in a budget night media release. He was the Minister, after all.

What allowed Brandis to do this? In a word: power.

Power is a much-abused term. That doesn't mean it's

not relevant to our examination. So let's examine political power in Australia, using the example of cultural policy. Power is a subtle and chameleonic thing. The philosopher Stephen Lukes thinks it is 'three-dimensional'. The sociologist Michael Mann thinks it is about 'power resources.' Max Weber called power 'the chance of a man or of a number of men to realize their own will in a communal action even against the resistance of others.'[29] It is the ability to exert your will on others that the powerful actor enjoys. It is perfectly comprehensible to all those exerting it or subjected to it. The vernacular idea of power as the ability of the powerful to exert dominance over others just about covers it. And it just so happens that the classic definition of power, by Weber, neatly approaches that idea.

Power is the great subject of journalism, and it is not surprising that many journalists default to realist (or quasi-realist) analyses. The journalist is granted the ability and privilege to see the workings of power close up. These can alternatively fascinate or revolt, but can hardly fail to impress. The apparatus of power, and the means with which it is deployed, remain absorbing subjects of human enquiry.

Of course it's more than this, because power is also consequential. The decisions of the powerful affect others, making and unmaking social contracts and communal relations. The stroke of the minister's pen can lead to job losses, companies closing and protests on the street. This sounds melodramatic–until you realise that all of these things have happened in the arts in the past year. I have attended Senate inquiries, witnessed street protests and watched arts ministers dissemble to a media pack. Culture is far more political than its own practitioners realise.

In contemporary Australian democracy, power is exercised in a number of ways. First and foremost, it is the prerogative of elected governments. The Department of Prime Minister and Cabinet remains the pre-eminent decision-making body in the Australian public service; together with the Finance and Treasury Departments, they make up the so-called 'central agencies.' Decisions about policy and money flow down the chain from a very constrained number of individuals—the Prime Minister, his senior advisors, the Treasurer, perhaps a couple of other senior ministers. Full Cabinet meetings are supposedly the seat of executive government, but nowadays key decisions are taken before the cabinet even sits. Kevin Rudd was notorious for making peremptory decisions in a 'kitchen cabinet' of just four (Rudd, Wayne Swan, Julia Gillard and Lindsay Tanner); Tony Abbott and Peta Credlin were often perceived as a duumvirate.

Decisions from the top flow down to the line departments, responsible for their various 'silos': Communications, Defence, Social Services, and eventually the Arts. Money for activities like funding artists is only grudgingly dispensed: the arts are not seen as a serious activity of the Australian Government, but rather a bell-and-whistle, an add-on, a bit of window dressing.[30] The small investment in culture in Australia—around about $650 million in the Arts portfolio, a little more than $2 billion if you include the ABC and SBS—is essentially a rounding error in the context of a $400 billion federal budget.

Within its reasonably traditional Weberian state bureaucracy, various policy spheres get treated separately and divisibly. Cultural policy is a good example. The Australia Council, nominally independent, receives its funding and imprimatur from the Arts Ministry. So do the national cultural institutions like the National Gallery and Library. The Arts Ministry is a little fiefdom of its own, with its own deputy-secretary and bureaucrats (though not many of them). It currently resides within the Communications Department, but in recent years it has been shuffled about between many different parent organisations, including the Prime Minister's Department, the Regional Development portfolio and the Attorney-General's Department, as befits its mendicant status. Other silos are located further afield. The ABC, arguably the single most important cultural institution of the Australian nation-state, pursues its own turbulent existence as a quasi-independent body within the Communications Department. Screen funding is disbursed through Screen Australia, but screen tax incentives devolve ultimately from the Treasury. Copyright and intellectual property rights belong to the Attorney-General. Australia does not have a single 'cultural czar'; even if we did, the Arts Minister would not be she.

Outside of the bureaucracy, power and influence course in different channels. Because government decisions can often make a difference to the future of whole industries, a sophisticated apparatus of lobbying and influence has sprung up in Canberra and around the major parties. There are no less than three major groups that purport to lobby for the interests of big business: the Business Council of Australia, representing the biggest companies; the Australian Chamber of Commerce and Industry, and the Ai Group. Influence-peddlers can also set themselves up as think-tanks, who work through a combination of political connection and engagement in the battle of ideas. On the right of politics, the paradigm example is of course the Institute for Public Affairs (IPA), but there are centrist and left-leaning think-tanks as well: the centrist Grattan Institute, the Labor-affiliated McKell Institute, the left-wing Australia Institute and the ostensibly Green Climate Institute, to name just four.[31]

This dense undergrowth of favour supports an entire class of para-bureaucrats and wonks. Industry bodies provide a channel for aggrieved interest groups to translate their concerns into policy action. Policy analysts write papers on particular issues, in the hope of bringing them to the attention of politicians and the media. Submissions to Parliamentary inquiries are researched and written. Opinion articles for the media are assiduously churned out. Much of this work is intellectual: the construction of arguments intended to sway the minds of policymakers and associated elites. Indeed, it can sometimes seem that the chief job of an IPA employee is punditry: opinion writing, or even simply opinion saying, filling the screens and airwaves with politically-themed media content.

Soft power is one thing. But it's no match for hard power. And within his domain as the Arts Minister, George Brandis did wield hard power. As Attorney-General, Brandis was the highest elected lawman in the country. Within the apparatus of the Australian public service, ministerial power remains swift and absolute. George Brandis knew that, and he used it to great effect. The man who had moved an amendment to the Australia

Council reform bill to try and give the arts minister more power knew that he possessed the prerogative of executive power, and he used it. It was Brandis' decision to create a National Program for Excellence in the Arts, and to do it with the Australia Council's funding. The funding cuts to the smaller companies of Black Friday were the inevitable and direct result.

8. The long shadow of neoliberalism

Why had the arts proved such a vulnerable target? The answer has to do with the development of cultural norms and political power structures in broader Australian society.

It will not come as news to Australia's scientists and environmentalists that the assault on the independence and integrity of arts funding was part of a broader offensive on public-interest broadcasting, science and education. The bowdlerised neoliberalism of this Coalition government is notable for its open hostility to policies of public funding for the arts, for science, for broadcasting and for the universities.[32] There were times during 2013 and 2014 in which Abbott and his Conservative ministers seemed more interested in fighting culture wars than in governing the country. Their chief target was all too often the ideal of the public good or the broader commons. There were concerted efforts to attack the independence of publicly-funded research centres and programs. Funding was cut to the CSIRO, to the ARC, to the Commonwealth Antarctic program, and the Government tried to abolish the Australian Renewable Energy Agency and the Clean Energy Finance Corporation, but was stymied in the Senate. There have been significant cuts to the ABC in this term of Government, totalling around $355 million cumulatively.[33]

The attacks on the Australia Council are of a piece with these other assaults against the public sphere. As with climate science and the universities, the target is those remnant sections of Australian society that still support or endorse non-market values. Science is valuable for many reasons, including the astonishing transformations it has made in the lives of ordinary people, but the practice of science values curiosity above economic gain. In the case of climate change, this has produced a body of work that fundamentally challenges the logic of the market. But perhaps the most dangerous challenge is that posed by science's internal logic, which values the testing of hypotheses by evidence, and is not necessarily inclined to subscribe to the neoliberal view that the only goal of government is economic growth, to be achieved by the insinuation of market forces into every remaining crevice of everyday life.[34]

Similarly, in contemporary Australia, universities still profess to pursue education for its own sake. But they are increasingly governed by a recondite set of rules and managerial policies that drive their interactions with students. The Australian Government openly encourages universities to compete against each other, for student enrolments, research grants and for highly-prized rankings on proliferating university league tables. Increasingly, academics are ranked and monitored through a set of metrics and indices, such as publication outcomes, citation records, student evaluation scores and the amount of research income they bring in. Students are openly described as 'customers', and courses are characterised as 'products.' The justification for university education has changed, too. In place of the soaring Victorian rhetoric of John Henry Newman's 'idea of the university', the value of education is now expressed in economic terms.[35] Thus, as the universities themselves argue to the federal government, the reason the taxpayer should fund students to study at university is not to become better educated, but because graduates boost productivity growth, earn more income over their lifetimes, and therefore increase the future wealth of the nation.[36]

Such examples of what Philip Mirowski has called 'everyday neoliberalism'[37] reveal the increasingly inhospitable intellectual climate for the public support of culture. For instance, no-one seems to think it a problem that the chairman of the Sydney Theatre Company is Ian Narev, the CEO of a major bank. What does a banker know about theatre? In a neoliberal world, business know-how is transferrable to any cultural endeavour. But would an actor ever be appointed chair of the Commonwealth Bank? Imagine the howls of outrage if the reverse of the Australia Council Review process had occurred: if, say, a visual artist and a festival director were asked by government to chair an inquiry into the banking sector. The scenario is revealingly improbable.

It was the Biennale boycott that made such contradictions impossible to ignore. Not only had artists shown themselves to be motivated by an animus against government policy—and there was no more treasured policy of the Abbott Government than the mandatory offshore detention of asylum seekers—but also against the values of the market itself. For this they would be punished.

9. How to fight taxes and change prime ministers

What should an industry do, when threatened by government fiat?

A vivid example was demonstrated in 2010, when the Rudd Government attempted to introduce a new tax on the profits of mining companies.

The Research Super Profits Tax emerged from the Henry Tax Review of 2010. It was framed by Treasury Secretary Ken Henry as a way of sharing the windfall profits of the huge iron ore and coal operations in Western Australia and Queensland, which at the time were creaming off billions from the sky-high commodity prices. Sensible enough in theory, the tax was sprung on the mining industry just months out from a federal election, and without much in the way of consultation, or even warning.

The reaction from the mining industry was swift. Over $20 million dollars—more than the advertising budget for either major party for an entire election—was poured into a media campaign against the tax. The mining industry body, the Minerals Council of Australia, coordinated a barrage of radio, television, cinema and online advertisements savaging the tax proposal. Every communication sheeted the blame home to Labor and Kevin Rudd.

According to Australian Electoral Commission filings, the Minerals Council spent $17.2 million, mainly on television commercials, while BHP Billiton spent $4.2 million and Rio Tinto more than half a million.[38] In the West, the confected anger ran white hot; Fortescue's Andrew Forrest, wearing high-vis, famously addressed a public rally from the back of a flat-bed truck.

'We represent so much more than mining,' Forrest thundered.

> *We represent the hopes and dreams of thousands and millions of people who depend on the mining industry, who depend on the resource sector for a strong Australian economy. This day is about your opportunity to change Australia's history from where Kevin Rudd would take it, a largely socialist distribution of capital over creation of value.*[39]

The 'axe the tax' protest on 9 June 2010 was only 1,200 strong—evidence perhaps that the issue was by no means as unpopular as it seemed—but the television pictures looked terrible for the Government.

The mining magnates didn't stop at protests. They wasted no time hiring the top advertising talent in the land: creative guru Neil Lawrence, the man who had crafted the Kevin 07 election campaign. The gusher of mining money paid for saturation coverage across mainstream broadcasting, in print and in social media—flooding the channels. Lawrence shot a series of arty television commercials, often featuring first-person stories of mining industry workers like truck drivers and miners. The spots were unusually long—sometimes even 90 seconds on prime-time television. They showed glossy portrayals of contented miners and engineers raising families, and contributing to their local communities. Olympic cyclist Anna Meares featured. Longer versions were available on a handsome website, ThisIsOurStory.com.au. Lawrence also came up with a three-word slogan, 'Keep Mining Strong', to devastating effect. Allies in the mainstream media, particularly the Murdoch newspapers, joined in.

The mining campaign, and Kevin Rudd's increasingly disorganised handling of it, rapidly degenerated into a full-blown crisis for the Labor Government. Already drifting in the polls after Rudd's abrupt decision to backflip on the 'great moral challenge' of climate change and abandon carbon pricing, the mining campaign smashed into a Party seething with discontent over the abrasive management style of its leader. As backbench supporters started to defect from the Rudd camp, senior factional leaders panicked and decided to replace Rudd with his deputy, Julia Gillard.

The knifing of an elected Prime Minster was the Labor Party's doing, and no-one else's. But it is difficult to believe Rudd would have been deposed if not for the disastrous blunder on mining. It was hard to disagree with journalist and author George Megalogenis when he argued in the 2013 SBS documentary *Dirty Business: How Mining Made Australia* that 'the mining industry [...] were the catalyst for [Rudd's] demise.'[40] In Gillard's very first media conference, the new Prime Minister announced that 'fixing' the mining tax was one of her top priorities. 'Today, I am throwing open the government's door to the mining industry,' Gillard said, 'and in return I ask the mining industry to open its mind.'[41]

10. The silence of the Australia Council

The mining tax campaign of 2010 showed what real power looked like for an Australian industry in the twenty-first century. Power like this—real power, the power to help bring down an elected leader—is something the arts and cultural industries can only dream about.

Indeed, any comparison between the response by the arts sector to the Excellence Raid and that of the anti-mining tax campaign is ridiculous. While the mining industry could marshal millions, command airwaves and influence the ruling party to dump the nation's prime minister, the arts and cultural sector's reaction was impotent.

The collective reaction to the Brandis raid was shock, followed by panic, and then retreat into hiding. In the shell-shocked wake of the Excellence decision in May 2015, artists around the country waited for the sector's leaders to mobilise against the changes. And waited. From the time of Whitlam, the arms-length principle of arts funding had underpinned Australian cultural policy. Surely now the Australia Council would speak out? But the silence was palpable.

For working artists, the silence from the established leaders of the Australian cultural sector in response to the cuts was the cruellest cut. For many, it seemed unbelievable that an arts minister could do this. For an industry that regularly mounts productions of *Richard III*, *Antigone* and the Ring Cycle, its ignorance of the way power works is puzzling. The naivety of the Australian arts sector was exposed.

Most shocking was the supine attitude of the Australia Council itself. The Australia Council is a supposedly independent government agency, entrusted by its governing legislation with the functions of 'uphold[ing] and promot[ing] freedom of expression in the arts' and 'promot[ing] the appreciation, knowledge and understanding of the arts.'[42] Looking at the smoking ruins of the Australia Council's independence in 2016, it's hard to argue that the current board and management of the Australia Council have fulfilled those duties.

Why did the Australia Council's board stay so quiet? The Australia Council's chair, the plutocratic Rupert Myer, has preferred to work in the backrooms, lobbying ministers and politicians at the level to which he is privy. Some attribute the removal of Brandis as Arts Minister to Myer's superb connections amongst Australia's ruling elite. But publicly, so far, nothing has been said. In 2015 I had a phone conversation with Australia Council board member Waleed Aly about the Australia Council's funding cut. The contents of the discussion are off the record, but Aly's public record on Australia Council funding is plain enough: there is none. The Gold Logie winner could have been the arts sector's most eloquent spokesperson: after all, he has his own television show. But at the time of writing, he had so far declined to publicly defend the agency. Much the same could be said for deputy chair Robyn Archer, whose statements about the funding cuts have been equivocal, to say the least.

Whatever the nuances, the silence of its board has left the Australia Council with few public defenders. A different membership might have acted differently in response to the unprecedented attack; it's difficult to imagine Donald Horne, when he was Chair, staying silent if this had happened on his watch. But nothing has come to pass. In response to the wholesale assault on the organisation's statutory independence, the Australia Council rolled over.

The Brandis raid also exposed faultlines between the various sub-sectors of the arts. The people who should have been defending the Australia Council, volubly and with considerable influence, were the supremos of the 28 major performing arts institutions: their board members and chairs, many of them big donors to the Liberal Party itself. Given that they had been quarantined from the funding cuts, they arguably had nothing to lose. Moreover, in figures like Richard Tognetti and Lyndon Terracini, the majors had media-savvy impresarios who could have been counted on to get themselves plenty of airtime.

But in the climate of fear (or was it indifference?) that Brandis' funding raid induced, the major performing arts companies largely stayed silent. A few isolated figures spoke out, like Black Swan's then director Kate Cherry, Queensland Theatre Company's Wesley Enoch and State Theatre Company of South Australia's Geordie Brookman. In contrast, Opera Australia callously welcomed the changes, and other artistic directors said nothing. Ordinary artists have been forced to admit that they had surrendered much of their day-to-day dealings with government to arts administrators and so-called 'cultural leaders', only to discover that these dear leaders may not have had their best interests at heart.

It was also clear that, whatever the attitudes of the 'cultural leaders', there wasn't much of a campaign infrastructure with which to fight the decision. The mining sector had shown what could be achieved by deep pockets and saturation campaigning. But since Brandis' decision was ultimately one of executive prerogative, the champions of Australian culture were left with little option but to oppose Brandis with guerilla tactics, improvised on the run.

Given the proliferation of industry associations, peak bodies, think-tanks and lobby firms in Canberra, the absence of any real advocacy voice for culture in Australia is conspicuous. Until a year ago, there was no peak body of any kind for the arts sector, let alone one representing the broader cultural industries. The peak body that eventually emerged, ArtsPeak, is weak and poorly-resourced. This reflects the fact that the various smaller industry representatives are typically part-time and rather sheltered affairs. Groups representing particular art forms, like the National Association for the Visual Arts or AusDance, are often little more than an executive director and a couple of office workers. Many are hobbled by absurdly small catchments: the Australian Society of Authors represents the authors of books, but not journalists or freelance writers. The Confederation of Australian State Theatre Companies represents the mainstage state theatres, but not the smaller performing arts companies. The Media Arts and Entertainment Alliance does represent cultural workers across the sector, but the atomised and casualised nature of the industry makes it a relatively weak trade union.

The group representing the major performing arts companies, AMPAG, is better resourced and much better connected. But the best-resourced bodies are in fact the collection agencies—the legal cartels set up to manage copyright royalties. These are a mix of ruthless industry power politics and more enlightened policy advocacy. While the songwriting agency APRA-AMCOS is the richest and therefore the most benign of the copyright cartels, the music publishing body PPCA seems to spend most of its time litigating against hapless industries like gyms that play music to their customers. Even so, there is no dedicated think-tank for the arts and culture, so little alternative policy is developed. This leaves the industry disadvantaged when the Productivity Commission puts out a major report on copyright reform, for example. It also means there is little in the way of push-back when the Arts Ministry or the Australia Council announces their latest strategy or reorganisation. The result is a weak and fearful industry, often unwilling and unable to argue for its own value.

As Meyrick wrote in 2014,

> *the British politician Lord Hailsham coined the phrase 'elective dictatorship' to describe the drift of modern democracies towards centralized control. Artists have been part of this drift, supposing we could take the money and recognition but avoid the pernicious logic and its effects.*[43]

It's not that the arts lobby brings a knife to a gunfight. It's more that the arts doesn't even know it's about to be beaten up.

11. Getting political: Free the Arts and the anti-Brandis resistance

Into this vacuum sprang a spontaneous grassroots protest, catalysed from the base by a motley crew of smaller arts companies. While the bigger organisations remained silent, and many feared to speak up, a group of artists and activists from the grassroots of the cultural sector took up the fight. Successive waves of funding cuts and the drive of federal cultural policy away from support for the Australia Council galvanised a cohort of arts advocates to organise a hurried attempt at resistance.

What followed was an example of what can happen when the sector mobilises its innate creativity in the absence of money and power. Instead of national advertising, the arts sector improvised a surprisingly effective social media campaign. The slogan Free the Arts ended up as a hashtag, and then became a Facebook page. Then followed the subversive genius of the 'George Brandis Live Art Experience', which made satirical memes of the hapless Arts Minister.[44]

Finally, and perhaps most significantly, there were on-the-ground public protests in five capital cities, with the largest protest held in Melbourne on the forecourt of the Australian Centre for Contemporary Art. These protests were widely covered by the mainstream media and focused attention on the Excellence Raid. For perhaps the first time, the small-to-medium sector organised a formal lobbying visit to Canberra, to meet with Labor, Greens and cross-bench senators.

Resistance also arose from the unlikely origin of the Senate cross-bench, which took an interest in the Brandis funding cuts after the Excellence controversy blew up in May. The support from cross-benchers like Independent Senator Glenn Lazarus allowed Labor and the Greens to get up a Senate inquiry into the Brandis changes. This set the scene for the spectacle of the Inquiry travelling around the country, gathering evidence about the value of the small-scale and independent cultural sector. The final report detailed evidence from no fewer than 2,200 submissions, and hundreds of hours of testimony in hearings held in most of the capital cities. The Senate report recommended restoring the Australia Council's funding and abandoning the Excellence Program.[45] It was largely ignored by the Government, of course. But it played a galvanising role in the anti-Brandis protests throughout the country.

The fascinating thing about this resistance was the bottom up, democratic nature of it. In the absence of any support from the large cultural institutions—too timid to speak up, too compromised by their compacts with powerful elites—the campaign was led by a small group of community artists, such as Norm Horton and Sarah Moynihan of Brisbane community arts company Feral Arts, Jade Lillie of the Footscray Community Arts

Centre, and the indefatigable Tamara Winikoff at the National Association for the Visual Arts. In contrast to the phoney 'cultural leadership' exemplified by the Australia Council, the incipient movement stayed close to its roots and concentrated on mobilising ordinary artists via social media and campaigns on the ground.

They were helped from an unexpected direction. The "save live Australian music" or SLAM movement in inner-city Melbourne. In its opposition to Melbourne's liquor licensing and lockout laws in 2010, this ginger group had shown itself to be the most effective campaigner on cultural issues in the country. Led by music producers Helen Marcou and Quincy McLean of the Bakehouse Studios, the SLAM organisers had worked for years to defeat Victoria's anti-music regulations and noise laws. Marcou and McLean set up the SLAM rally of February 2010, in which an estimated 20,000 Melbournians rallied on the steps of Victorian Parliament in support of live music, and made cultural policy a live election issue in the 2010 Victorian race. SLAM had shown that grassroots activism could make politicians sit up and listen: now Marcou would share some of her secrets with the Free the Arts organisers.[46]

As is so often the case in politics, the most important thing was not the size or impact of the resistance (although this was considerable), but the fact that there was resistance at all. The critical result was that Brandis and the Excellence program were contested, even while the Australia Council and the major cultural companies stayed quiet.

In September 2015, Brandis was dumped as Arts

Minister by Malcolm Turnbull, and replaced with Mitch Fifield. Fifield announced he would rebrand the Excellence fund as 'Catalyst', and return some of the money to the Australia Council. It was a partial victory at best: most of the Australia Council funding cuts had been locked in by the original decision, and the fate of the Australia Council still looked precarious. But there is little doubt that without the opposition of Free the Arts and the small-to-medium sector, George Brandis would still be the Arts Minister, and the Australia Council would be in even greater peril.

11. An idea for championing Australian culture

In the run-up to the 2016 election, the Australia Council now finds itself in a dangerous place. There is little love on the Coalition backbench for the organisation, and the election of a second-term Turnbull Government could well signal the beginning of the end for the agency. It is not a good sign that so many of the arts administrators I regularly talk to appear convinced that the Australia Council will be abolished altogether should Turnbull win.

If that does happen, one of the key causes of its downfall will be the strange timidity of so many in Australian culture to speak up in their own defence. Why is this? The question that the board of the Australia Council was so fearful of addressing—the cause from which it had shirked its responsibility for advocating—was in fact the age-old one, perhaps the only one that counts for the current conversation: Why fund the arts?

This is a critical question for the sector. Surprisingly, little overt effort has been made to answer it. One reason may be that many in the arts are simply unable to get their voices heard. Another may be that we lack the appropriate language with which to tell this story.

I want to spend a little time advancing an argument for why there should be funding for the arts, and why culture is important. This is an argument that could be taken up by the sector, by artists and arts administrators, by campaigners, and by the putative national peak body and cultural policy think-tank that Australian culture so desperately needs.

Why fund the arts? The answer, for those who cared to listen, was recounted at Gough Whitlam's funeral, notable for the eulogy given by Noel Pearson. There, Cate Blanchett also gave a speech, in which she pointed to Whitlam's sage words on the value of the arts. On coming to office in 1972, Whitlam had championed a role for the arts and culture in a way unheard from an Australian leader since Alfred Deakin, and which has rarely been matched:

> *In any civilised community, the arts and associated amenities must occupy a central place. Their enjoyment should not be seen as remote from everyday life. Of all the objectives of my government, none had a higher priority than the encouragement of the arts—the preservation and enrichment of our cultural and intellectual heritage. Indeed I would argue that all other objectives of a Labor government—social reform, justice and equity in the provision of welfare services and educational opportunities—have as their goal the creation of a society in which the arts and the appreciation of spiritual and intellectual values can flourish. Our other objectives are all means to an end. The enjoyment of the arts is an end in itself.*[47]

The arts, Whitlam reminds us, are an end in themselves.

They are not a way station on the path to the greater good. They *are* the good—the good in and of itself—and so, logically, deserve the support extended to them by the begrudging taxpayer as the ultimate purpose of paying taxes.

Needless to say, this is not necessarily a view held by the full plurality of Australian society. In fact, it's fair to say that the idea of arts funding has some assiduous enemies in both major parties, and in many sections of the public service. From the perspective of the modern conservative or the libertarian, the need for public funding for the arts is self-evidently illusory. As the American economist Tyler Cowen has written, 'many of my conservative and libertarian friends find government funding of the arts unacceptable.'[48] For the neoliberal warriors at the IPA, the Australia Council is the paradigm case for the sort of thing the Government should abolish. After all, is it not the case that the market can provide plenty of artistic goods and services? Why should the taxpayer subsidise their provision? Why ever should the State get involved?

From this standpoint, arts funding is not just profoundly wasteful, but simply nonsensical. If artists want to embark on a career painting or writing or choreographing experimental dance theatre, then let them. But let them do it under their own steam, winning audiences and patrons for their work if they can. If they cannot earn an income from their work, let us not give other people's money in order to compensate them. Above all (runs this argument) do not force citizens, through the impost of taxation, to subsidise artists' follies.

This is a powerful position, and one with which a

great many people in our society agree. It behoves any would-be champion of public subsidy of the arts to take it seriously. If we support arts funding, we should answer this criticism in good faith, and develop useful arguments that contradict and perhaps even disprove it.

In crafting a response, the advocate can find herself on difficult terrain. If she is not careful, she can find herself boiling everything down to empty abstract concepts like 'excellence', 'beauty' and 'truth', when in fact there are sensible and practical reasons to support the arts and culture that are closer to street level. A few gifted artists really are virtuosi, but this is not the only reason to support culture. Beauty and truth can indeed be properties of many works of art, but justifying this to a sceptical arts minister or campaigning tabloid newspaper can be a tricky business. Faced with this difficulty, it can be tempting to stick with the established terms of current policy debates, and stress the benefits of arts funding in economic terms: creating jobs, earning exports and supporting the growth of cultural industries. As the British academic Philip Schlesinger said in 2015, 'I have been increasingly struck by how difficult it is *not* to talk about the creative industries and creative economy, and I want to argue that this has become both a conceptual and practical obstacle to thinking about culture and the complexity of cultural work.'[49]

There is great peril in phrasing cultural debates in economic language. Like Schlesinger and Monash University's Justin O'Connor (whose Platform Paper 47, *After the Creative Industries: Why we need a cultural economy* makes this point better than I can here).[50] I also think playing the 'creative industries' card is a bad idea. The economic weight of culture is of course increasingly important in a modern post-industrial society. But if the arts advocate chooses to engage on the instrumental ground of economic advantage, she will face many disappointments. The problem is that arts funding is simply not supportable on most readings of mainstream economic theory. An industry that needs constant subsidy is not really an industry at all, runs this analysis. It's a band of beggars. Funding the arts is understood by neoclassical economics as the provision of symbolic welfare: fireworks and circuses to amuse and placate the masses, activity that could easily be carried out by the market. And that is in fact the way that Australian policymakers generally look at the arts sector: as a mendicant sector seeking handouts, manifestly unable to command economic advantage under its own sail. Even left-leaning politicians often place the provision of culture well down the list of state priorities, below the provision of pensions, schools and hospitals.

It is true that for some sections of the arts, particularly the smaller and more precarious sections, there is no convincing business model. Shorn of funding, many of these companies would fold, and the artists working for them would be forced back to working day jobs. If your view of culture is that any desire for it can easily be satisfied by the goods and services for sale in the global marketplace, then you are unlikely to be worried at the fate of such artistic practices.

There is no doubt about it: as Keynes recognised, many types of art and culture are by their nature unprofitable, and cannot be easily supported by ticket sales or subscriptions in the absence of public funding or private philanthropy (or a combination a both). The examples of the art museum or the public library are good ones: in 2016, it is not economically sensible to buy a prime block of real estate in the middle of a capital city, build a substantial building on it, fill it with books or expensive works of art, and then expect to make a profit from charging admission. But the same could be said for many smaller and more local activities: the community theatre collective, the poetry magazine, the festival of youth arts. None of these types of cultural activity seem likely to be profitable, as can be seen by the singular lack of multinational corporations plying a trade in experimental dance or chamber opera.

The funny thing about economic thinking of this sort is that, paradoxically but entirely predictably, massive Hollywood movie studios *do* qualify for government handouts under this kind of policy-making framework. This is because however much the boffins in Treasury may hate it, the sheer size and sophistication of global entertainment multinationals enables them to bargain hard with the nation-state over their level of investment. A $200 million location budget is something that, even if looked down upon by doctrinaire economists, any government minister can readily understand. After all, the thing about 'runaway production', as film scholars call it, is that it can run away to the part of the world that offers the most incentives.[51] In contrast, a blockbuster lured to Australia is a windfall gain that can be sold to the Finance and Treasury department gatekeepers as an investment that would not otherwise have occurred. It is therefore a carrot that can secure considerable government investment, in Mitch Fifield's case $47 million worth that he found literally by selling off Screen Australia's farm.[52]

In contrast, convincing ministers and economic bureaucrats of the need for the arts, as they exist in this country—particularly that unprofitable substrata of the local, the community, the experimental and the weird—is a decidedly tougher endeavour. There are schools under-funded, hospitals requiring imaging machines, and potholes on the roads. All are far more worthy objectives for public investment than nude photographs, unlovely art installations or slam poetry tournaments.

At this point, the knowledgeable policy expert—and perhaps the odd artist or two, on the odd occasion when they are allowed a say in such debates—replies that the funds expended on the arts are miniscule compared to those devoted to schools, roads and hospitals, and hence not truly comparable. The entire Australia Council's annual budget would buy just one Joint Strike Fighter; certainly not an Air Warfare Destroyer or a submarine. Public finance is about making choices, and the arts can be sacrificed without making any meaningful impact on the federal deficit, so large is that considerable sum ($37 billion in May 2016).[53] Given that the arts represent only a drop in the $400 billion budget ocean, why not simply fund them at present levels in perpetuity, and get on with the real business of government?

This has been a convenient view for the supporters of the arts to take—but a dangerous one. To argue that the arts should be funded because no-one would much notice if they weren't is not a great endorsement. More seriously, it invites legitimate criticism that the arts are not therefore worthy recipients of funding—that they are simply special interest pleaders.

It takes considerably more courage than this to take the more honest strategy of arguing for arts funding in and of itself. Perhaps this is because, in the contemporary moment, asserting a non-monetary value of any good or service is a seriously destabilising act. Art can be bought and sold, mass-produced and exploited, but much that is best in art and culture is so self-evidently non-monetary that it is obvious even to lay people that it can't be judged by the same yardstick as property values, stock options or commodity prices.

By their nature, their history and their example, the arts stand in colourful protest against the dominance of market forces (even if they provide lively instances of market activity); they are living proof of a higher good that makes policymakers, not to mention politicians, distinctly uncomfortable. Artists are a motley crew at the best of times, but it is also true that they harbour few illusions about the mathematical inevitability of Pareto efficiency. Worse, they are often hostile to the interests of capital, even while demanding patronage. Such 'vicious ingratitude', as Turnbull said of the artists boycotting the 2014 Sydney Biennale, outrages the captains of industry and well-heeled scions of inherited fortune who dominate the board rooms of ASX 200 companies.

So what is the way forward?

It turns out there are some rather good arguments for public support for the arts that need not slide into cultural elitism on the one hand, or special pleading and magical thinking on the other. In fact, the arts do have value, as the immense amount of enjoyment that they give millions of ordinary citizens every day shows. The argument is scarcely new—Aristotle articulated it 2,500 years ago—but in the current intellectual zeitgeist it is a newly radical proposition.

The Australian Bureau of Statistics has collected fascinating data that makes this point. In 2013–14, 15.9 million Australians aged over the age of 15 attended a cultural venue or event—or 86 per cent of all Australians in that age bracket. Table 1 below sets out some of the ABS data.

Table 1. Australians over the age of 15 attending a cultural venue or event, 2013-14.
Source: Australian Bureau of Statistics.[54]

Cultural venu e or event	Attendance (m)
Art galleries	4.98
Museums	5.19
Zoological parks and aquariums	6.27
Botanic gardens	6.87
Libraries	6.29
Archives	0.62
Performing arts	
Classical music concerts	1.64
Popular music concerts	6.03
Theatre performances	2.96
Dance performances	1.81

Musicals and operas	2.74
Other performing arts	3.19
Total attending at least one performance event	3.08
Cinemas	3.82
Total attending at least one cultural venue or event	5.02
(Total population aged 15 years and over)	(5.93)

Of course, not everyone who turns up to a cultural event enjoys themselves. But millions do.

The participation figures for culture in this country are striking, and deserve special examination. They show that around a quarter of all Australians make art or engage in artistic creativity. According to the Bureau's long-running survey, 'participation in selected cultural activities', nearly five million Australians in 2013–14 spent time participating in the 'performing arts, singing or playing a musical instrument, dancing, writing, visual art activities and craft activities.'[55] Australians also like making and supporting the arts: in 2006, Australian volunteered 30.6 million hours in arts and heritage organisations; another ABS survey in 2010 found that some 410,000 Australians volunteered for cultural organisations.[56]

Table 2. Australians over the age of 15 participating in a cultural activity, 2013-14.
Source: Australian Bureau of Statistics.

Cultural activity	Participants
Performing in a drama, comedy, opera or musical, including rehearsals	283,300
Performing in a cabaret or variety act, including rehearsals	101,000
Singing or playing a musical instrument	962,300
Dancing	618,500
Writing song lyrics, or mixing or composing music, including digital composition	467,200
Writing any fiction or non-fiction, such as stories, poetry or scripts	1,033,300
Sculpting, painting, drawing or cartooning, including digital pieces	1,538,300
Printmaking, screen printing or etching	227,600
Photography, film-making or editing, apart from recording personal events	1,015,700
Textile crafts, jewellery making, paper crafts or wood crafts	1,808,700
Glass crafts, pottery, ceramics or mosaics	293,900
Designing websites, computer games or interactive software	623,900
Fashion, interior or graphic design	421,300
Total participants	4,944,600
Total non-participants	13,537,600

When you examine these statistics, the surprisingly widespread devotion of ordinary Australians to cultural pursuits comes into focus. Far more Australians engage in culture than engage in politics. More Australians make art or culture than play organised sport. More Australians attend an art gallery annually than attend a football game. And yet, the crude stereotype remains of the arts as a marginal, disreputable and even pathetic activity. The truth is the polar opposite: that engagement with culture is one of the foundation stones of Australian civic life. This argument sometimes goes by the name 'public value.'[57] While there is plenty of formal academic theory carried out under that banner, the phrase is useful for our purposes because it reminds us that culture happens in the public sphere.

This, then, provides one powerful potential argument for state support of culture: the democratic value of cultural participation. The fact that the majority of the citizens of the Australian State share a vivid and rich cultural involvement, means that culture is not some way-station on the road to the good life. It *is* the good life, a vision of a modern society where much of the meaning and value derived by individuals and families is expressed through cultural and artistic participation and creation. As John Holden put it, back in 2006, a policy that supports publicly-funded culture can be one in which 'culture is seen as an integral and essential part of civil society.'[58] This is a vision in which the state supports culture because it enriches civic, social and public values, and because it is central to who we are as modern Australians. It is a vision that is democratic and collective, because it enriches not merely separate individuals, but the common good. It is a vision for culture that shares much of what is valuable in other domains of the human spirit: in religion, in education, and in the humanities. As the British political scientist Adam Roberts pointed out in 2010, these activities 'explore what it means to be human: the words, ideas, narratives and the art and artefacts that help us make sense of our lives and the world we live in; how we have created it and are created by it.'[59]

12. Anzac and the power of cultural symbols

In the cramped and fearful language that has marked the 2016 election campaign, such a capacious vision for culture seems unlikely, perhaps even utopian. But, with just a little investigation, it is possible to find a shining recent example of public support for cultural endeavour.

Since the mid-2000s, the Howard, Rudd, Gillard and Abbott governments have pursued one cultural policy with admirable consistency: the Centenary of Anzac. The Centenary of Anzac supported a widespread and long-running cultural program of events, which included major funding for the Australian War Memorial, the Shrine of Remembrance and other major galleries and museums, as well as money for a slew of commemorative events across the nation. Major state ceremonies in Australia and Turkey were coordinated across continents on 25 April, and commemorations continue with major ceremonies planned for 2016 in France to remember the courage of Australia's servicemen at the Battle of the Somme.

This was an explicit government policy, endorsed and re-endorsed by successive federal governments, planned for several years, and supported to the tune of more than half a billion dollars of taxpayer's money. The policy was pursued with no expectation of economic outcome, and yet championed enthusiastically by both major political parties, and most enthusiastically by the Coalition.

When Tony Abbott stood on the beach at Anzac Cove in Gelibolu in Turkey on 25 April last year, he enjoined us to commemorate an occasion of national cultural significance, in terms saturated in the language of moral virtue. Remembering Gallipoli was important, Abbott told us, because 'we believe that the Anzacs represented Australians at our best'.

> *It's the perseverance of those who scaled the cliffs under a rain of fire.*
>
> *It's the compassion of the nurses who attended to the thousands of wounded.*
>
> *It's the conquest of fear, often through a larrikin sense of humour.*
>
> *And it's the greatest love anyone can have: the readiness to lay down your life for your friend.*[60]

There is much to decry in the celebration of death in war as 'the greatest love anyone can have', and it is not my intention here to praise Abbott's nationalistic sentiments. But his insistence on the moral purpose of Gallipoli is revealing. Here is one policy of government that has nothing to do with economic utility. The justification for commemorating Anzac has always and only been cultural and moral, from Charles Bean to Tony Abbott. Indeed, Australian law sacralises the memory of the Great War with a specific law prohibiting the commercialisation of the word 'Anzac'. Anzac shows that the arguments for culture in and of itself can be powerful forces in the intellectual life of a nation.[61]

There was nothing in Abbott's speech about the need for remembering the Great War to drive tourism, to boost economic growth, or to provide jobs.[62] The reason that Anzac should be remembered, he argued, was that the ethical conduct of Australian and New Zealand soldiers provides a shining example to the men and women of Australia today. 'Duty, selflessness, moral courage,' Abbott concluded: 'always these remain the mark of a decent human being.'

From the unlikely inspiration of Tony Abbott, then, comes one cue for the way to champion culture. This is the idea that culture makes us a better person: the Arnoldian belief in 'the best which has been thought and said.'[63] But even if we don't subscribe to the view of art as a religion (or, in the case of Anzac, a secular cult), the moral power of Abbott's argument remains.

I don't agree with Tony Abbott: I don't believe the memory of war can help us be 'decent human beings.' It would be well to believe in an ethical mechanism whereby the memory of historical trauma creates more virtuous, or even more peaceful human beings. The melancholy testimony of history suggests otherwise. Nor do I believe that culture makes us better humans. Some who loved the arts were violent and cruel, while many with little of what we would today call 'cultural capital' were kind, generous and brave. The personal lives of artists have often been scandalous.[64]

The terms of the Anzac debate show us that it is possible to make a potent argument for the public value of culture. There is an aching need for symbolic belonging in the hearts of all of us. Culture can give us that. It can enlarge our understanding. It can broaden our horizons and deepen our knowledge of the human. It can enrich our social milieu and build our common bonds and connections. If we dare to use them, symbols are powerful. Culture in its bewildering diversity is not the only thing, or even the most important thing, but it is an utterly essential thing. It is impossible to imagine a life lived meaningfully in the world without culture. It is easy to imagine a world in which less art and fewer artists would lead to a poorer, nastier and more brutish existence.

This is the cultural value of which we need to convince our fellow citizens. It shouldn't be too difficult to convince them, for they are humans too.

Endnotes

1 Ben Eltham, 'Devastating' OzCo grants just the tip of the iceberg, *Crikey*, 23 May 2016, online at: http://www.crikey.com.au/2016/05/23/more-artists-to-miss-out-in-australia-council-grants-saga/

2 Funding decision cuts deep into design [media release], Australian Design Centre, 13 May 2016, online at https://australiandesigncentre.com/latestnews/media-release-funding-decision-cuts-deep-design/

3 A.A. Phillips, The Cultural Cringe, *Meanjin* 9(4) 1950: 299–302.

4 'The Coalition, on the other hand, sees the work of artists and arts professionals as something which is intrinsically worthwhile, one of the essential elements of a confident and sophisticated society, which is to be judged on its own merits—not by whether it serves some other political or public policy agenda.' George Brandis, 'Taking arts to the next level', *Australian*, 5 September 2013, online at http://www.theaustralian.com.au/arts/opinion/taking-arts-to-the-next-level/story-fn9n9z9n-1226710602311

5 Raymond Williams, *Keywords: a vocabulary of culture and society*, rev. ed. (London: Fontana, 1983), p. 87.

6 See Adam Kuper's fascinating intellectual history of the idea of culture as it developed in the discipline of anthropology: Adam Kuper, *Culture: the anthropologists' account* (Cambridge, MA: Harvard University Press, 1999).

7 Williams, *Keywords*, p. 90.

8 See, for instance, my study of experimental musicians: Ben Eltham, 'A "game of nomenclature"? Performance-based sonic practice in Australia', *Art*

Monthly Australia 225 (2009): 42-44.
9 *Creative Australia: National Cultural Policy* (Canberra: Australian Government, 2013), online at http://creativeaustralia.arts.gov.au/assets/Creative-Australia-PDF-20130417.pdf
10 Ben Eltham, 'Australian cultural and innovation policies: never the twain shall meet?', *Innovation: Management, Policy & Practice* 11 (2009): 230–239.
11 Gabrielle Trainor & Angus James, *Review of the Australia Council, May 2012* (Canberra: Ministry for the Arts, 2013).
12 Jo Porter and Rick Heath quotes taken from my report: Ben Eltham, 'Arts funding winners grin, but some criticism for Crean report', *Crikey*, 15 March 2013. online at http://www.crikey.com.au/2013/03/15/arts-funding-winners-grin-but-some-criticism-for-crean-report/
13 Emma Griffiths & Ben Atherton, 'As it happened: Gillard survives as challenge fizzles', ABC, 21 March 2013, online at http://www.abc.net.au/news/2013-03-21/live-coverage:-labor-leadership-crisis/4586250
14 Ben Eltham, 'My cup of tea: Crean's cultural policy in jeopardy', *Crikey*, 22 March 2013, online at http://www.crikey.com.au/2013/03/22/my-cup-of-tea-cultural-policy-in-jeopardy/
15 *Australia Council Act 2013* (Commonwealth of Australia).
16 Brandis quoted by Matthew Westwood, 'George Brandis details Coalition's arts manifesto', *Australian*, 20 August 2013, online at http://www.theaustralian.com.au/arts/george-brandis-details-coalitions-arts-manifesto/story-e6frg8n6-1226700080674
17 George Brandis, 'Taking arts to the next level', *Australian*, 5 September 2013, online at http://www.theaustralian.com.au/arts/opinion/taking-arts-to-the-next-level/story-fn9n9z9n-1226710602311
18 Ben Eltham, 'Sydney Biennale faces Transfield boycott threat', *Arts Hub*, 6 February 2014, online at http://www.artshub.com.au/news-article/feature/all-arts/sydney-biennale-faces-transfield-boycott-threat-198020
19 Michael Cathcart, 'Why did Belgiorno-Nettis resign from Sydney Biennale Board?', *Books and Arts*, ABC, 11 March 2014, online at http://www.abc.net.au/radionational/programs/booksandarts/why-did-belgiorno-nettis-resign-from-sydney-biennale-board3f/5311796
20 Lisa Cox, Andrew Taylor & Lucy Carroll, 'George Brandis urges penalty for arts organisations rejecting corporate sponsorship', *Sydney Morning Herald*, 15 March 2014, online at http://www.smh.com.au/national/george-brandis-urges-penalty-for-arts-organisations-rejecting-corporate-sponsorship-20140314-34s2v.html#ixzz4AC1jPBeK
21 Jonathan Swan, 'Malcolm Turnbull denounces "vicious ingratitude" of Biennale artists after Transfield withdraws as sponsor', *Sydney Morning Herald*, 11 March 2014, online at http://www.smh.com.au/federal-politics/political-news/malcolm-turnbull-denounces-vicious-ingratitude-of-biennale-artists-after-transfield-withdraws-as-sponsor-20140310-34ik6.html#ixzz4ABxNeK1j
22 H. C. Coombs in his 1973 Australia Council Chairman's Report, quoted in H. Guldberg, *The Arts Economy 1968-1998* (Sydney: Australia Council, 2000), p.85.
23 E. Gough Whitlam's Second Reading speech, Australia Council Bill, 23 July 1974, quoted in Arnaldo Barone, *A New Economic Theory of Public Support for the Arts* (London: Routledge, 2015), p.5.
24 John Maynard Keynes, 'Art and the State' (1936), in D. Moggridge (ed.), *The Collected Writings of John Maynard Keynes*, vol. 28, (London: Macmillan, 1982): 341–349.
25 John Gardiner-Garden, *Commonwealth arts policy and administration,*

Parliamentary Library Background Note, 7 May 2009. (Canberra: Parliamentary Library).

26 Julian Meyrick, 'Think before you move: the artist and the competitive grant system', August 2014, online at http://blogs.flinders.edu.au/laboratory-adelaide/2016/05/13/think-before-you-move/

27 Ben Eltham, 'The Excellence Criterion', *Overland* 211 (2015), online at https://overland.org.au/previous-issues/issue-221/feature-ben-eltham/

28 Biographical detail for James and Trainor taken from their *Review of the Australia Council*, pp. 38–39.

29 Theories of power: Stephen Lukes, *Power: a radical view* (New York: Palgrave Macmillan, 2005); Michael Mann, *The Sources of Social Power*, vol. 2 (Cambridge: Cambridge University Press, 1993).

30 The disdain held by central government ministries such as Treasury and the Prime Minister's Department has been well-documented, at least inside a state government, by Leigh Tabrett: *It's Culture, Stupid!: Reflections of an arts bureaucrat*, Platform Paper 34 (2013).

31 My discussion of Australian public policy is largely informed by my experience over a decade as a working journalist. In the academic literature, much the best treatment of this subject (including the role of think-tanks and lobby groups) is by Sarah Maddison & Richard Denniss, *An Introduction to Australian Public Policy: theory and practice* (Cambridge: Cambridge University Press, 2013).

32 As the sociologist Wendy Brown has noted in her fine recent book on neoliberalism, neoliberalism is 'a distinctive mode of reason, of the production of subjects, a "conduct of conduct," and a scheme of valuation.' Wendy Brown, *Undoing the Demos: Neoliberalism's stealth revolution.* (Brooklyn: Zone Books, 2015), p. 21.

33 ABC, 'Submission to the House of Representatives Standing Committee on Communications and the Arts, Inquiry into the importance of public and commercial broadcasting, online content and live production to rural and regional Australia, including the arts, news and other services' (Ultimo, NSW: ABC, February 2016).

34 The best discussion of the strange antipathy nurtured by neoliberalism towards universities, science and knowledge is by Philip Mirowski, *Never let a Serious Crisis go to Waste: how neoliberalism survived the financial meltdown* (London: Verso, 2013), pp. 81-83.

35 See Stefan Collini's discussion of Newman's idea of the university: *What Are Universities For?* (London: Penguin, 2012), pp. 39–60.

36 See for instance the submission of the 'sandstone' universities to the Gillard Government in 2011: The Group of Eight, *Submission to the Review of Higher Education Base Funding* (Turner, ACT: The Group of Eight, 2011).

37 Mirowski, *Serious Crisis*, pp. 89-159.

38 Figures taken from a Fairfax Media report by Mark Davis, 'A snip at $22m to get rid of PM,' *Sydney Morning Herald*, 2 February 2011, online at http://www.smh.com.au/business/a-snip-at-22m-to-get-rid-of-pm-20110201-1acgj.html

39 Andrew Forrest quoted in Chalpat Sonti, 'Axe the tax'—mining magnates see red', *Sydney Morning Herald*, 9 June 2010, online at http://www.smh.com.au/business/axe-the-tax--mining-magnates-see-red-20100609-xvqj.html

40 George Megalogenis quoted in the film directed by Jacob Hickey, *Dirty Business: how mining made Australia, Episode 2: Power*, Artamon NSW: SBS, 2013.

41 Julia Gillard quote taken from Fairfax Media report by Chris Zappone, 'Ceasefire between miners and government', *Sydney Morning Herald*, 24 June

2010, online at http://www.smh.com.au/business/ceasefire-between-miners-and-government-20100624-z14a.html#ixzz49k8h4ewl
42 *Australia Council Act 2013* (Commonwealth of Australia), s. 9.
43 Julian Meyrick, 'Think before you move'.
44 'The George Brandis Live Art Experience', online at https://www.facebook.com/TheGeorgeBrandisLiveArtExperience/
45 Senate Legal and Constitutional Affairs References Committee, *Impact of the 2014 and 2015 Commonwealth Budget decisions on the Arts* (Canberra: Department of the Senate, 2015).
46 I base this part of the essay on personal discussions with the arts advocates named in the text. See also Clinton Walker, *History is Made at Night: Live Music in Australia*, Platform Paper 32 (2012).
47 E. Gough Whitlam, *The Whitlam Government 1972-1975* (Ringwood, Vic: Viking, 1985) p. 553. Blanchett's speech was published as 'Cate Blanchett pays tribute to Gough Whitlam', *Sydney Morning Herald*, 5 November 2014, online at http://www.smh.com.au/comment/cate-blanchett-pays-tribute-to-gough-whitlam-full-text-20141105-11hdb1.html
48 Tyler Cowen, *Good and Plenty: the creative successes of American arts funding*, Princeton: Princeton University Press, 2006), p. 1.
49 Philip Schlesinger, 'The Creative Economy: invention of a global orthodoxy', public lecture, 25 November 2015 online at http://www.lse.ac.uk/publicEvents/events/2015/11/20151125t1830vHKT.aspx
50 Justin O'Connor, *After the Creative Industries: why we need a cultural economy*, Platform Paper 47 (2016).
51 Runaway screen production explored in Alex Burns & Ben Eltham, 'Boom and bust in Australian screen policy: 10BA, the Film Finance Corporation, and Hollywood's "race to the bottom" ', *Media international Australia* 136 (2010), pp. 103–18. The work of Janet Wasko has been central to this discussion. See: Janet Wasko & Mary Erickson (eds.), *Cross-Border Cultural Production: economic runaway or globalization?* (Amherst, NY: Cambria Press, 2008).
52 The 2015 Mid-Year Fiscal and Economic Outlook revealed that $35 million raised by the sale of Screen Australia's former production facility at Lindfield would be directed to subsidise the Australian location budget of two Hollywood feature films, *Alien: Covenant* and *Thor*: *Ragnarok*. See Luke Buckmaster, 'New Screen Australia Budget Cuts: how the government's deal with Hollywood treated us like mugs', *Daily Review*, 16 December 2015, online at https://dailyreview.com.au/new-screen-australia-budget-cuts-how-the-governments-deal-with-hollywood-treated-us-like-mugs/34823/
53 Department of Treasury, *Pre-Election Economic and Fiscal Outlook* (Canberra: Australian Government, 2016).
54 Australian Bureau of Statistics, *Attendance at Selected Cultural Venues and Events, Australia, 2013–14*. Cat. No. 4114.0 (Canberra: Australian Bureau of Statistics, 2015).
55 Australian Bureau of Statistics, *Participation in Selected Cultural Activities, Australia, 2013-14*. Cat. No. 4921.0 (Canberra: Australian Bureau of Statistics, 2015).
56 Figures quoted in *Arts and Culture in Australia: a statistical overview, 2014*. Cat. No. 4172.0 (Canberra: Australian Bureau of Statistics, 2014).
57 The literature on public value and its offshoot in cultural policy theory, 'cultural value', is vast. John Holden remains a key thinker. See John Holden, *Cultural Value and the crisis of legitimacy* (London: Demos, 2006); Dave O'Brien, *Measuring the value of culture* (London: Department of Media, Culture and Sport, 2010); and David John Lee, Kate Oakley & Richard

Naylor, ' "The public gets what the public wants"? The uses and abuses of "public value" in contemporary British cultural policy', *International Journal of Cultural Policy*, 17(3) (2011): 289–300.

58 John Holden, *Capturing Cultural Value.*

59 Adam Roberts, 'Introduction', *Past, Present and Future: the public value of Humanities and Social Sciences* (London: British Academy, 2010), p.2.

60 Sarah Kimmorley, 'Here's the touching speech Prime Minister Tony Abbott gave at the dawn service in Gallipoli', *Business Insider Australia*, 25 April 2015, online at http://www.businessinsider.com.au/heres-the-touching-speech-prime-minister-tony-abbott-gave-at-the-dawn-service-in-gallipoli-2015-4

61 Ken Inglis, *Sacred places: war memorials in the Australian landscape.* (Carlton, Vic.: Melbourne University Publishing, 2008).

62 In fact, Australian law sacralises the memory of Anzac with a specific law prohibiting the commercialisation of the word 'Anzac.'

63 Matthew Arnold, *Culture and Anarchy* (Cambridge: Cambridge University Press, 1932), p.6.

64 The most eloquent discussion of this dilemma is by John Carey, *What good are the arts?* (New York: Oxford University Press, 2005).

FORTHCOMING

PP No.49, November 2016
RETHINKING THE DOCUMENTARY
Curtis Levy

Throughout the history of cinema, Australia has produced many landmark documentaries but very few have been acclaimed in recent times. And yet there is a huge appetite for quality documentaries and substantial audiences flock to cinemas to see the work of others. What has happened to Australia's documentary filmmaking?

Veteran award-winning documentary maker Curtis Levy (*The President versus David Hicks*, *Hephzibah*) and recognized for his works on the politics of Indonesia, believes there is a disjunction between the taste dictated by the management of Australian media and that of their customers. He argues that the survival of documentaries in and about this country and the region must no longer be predicated on television ratings.

He calls for the whole subject of documentary making to be opened for discussion. Audiences and managers need to be blasted out of their comfort zones and risk new ways and new marketing. With greater awareness, we could sweep away for good the parochialism that pervades the documentary industry today.

Copyright Information

PLATFORM PAPERS
Quarterly essays from Currency House Inc.
Founding Editor: Dr John Golder
Currency House Inc. is a non-profit association and resource centre advocating the role of the performing arts in public life by research, debate and publication.

Postal address: PO Box 2270, Strawberry Hills, NSW 2012, Australia
Email: info@currencyhouse.org.au Tel: (02) 9319 4953
Website: www.currencyhouse.org.au Fax: (02) 9319 3649

ISBN 978 0 9924890 9-0
ISSN 1449-583X

Typeset in Garamond
Printed by McPherson's Printing Group
Production by XOU Creative